to

_____

with love

_____

date

_____

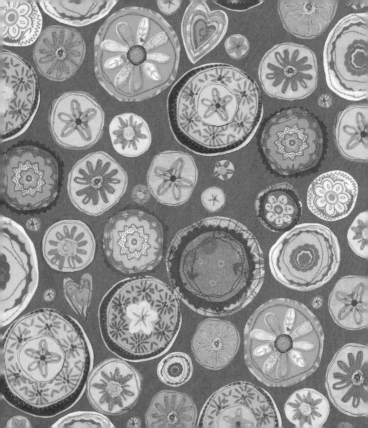

101 inspirational thoughts for MOM

Artwork by
lori siebert

HARVEST HOUSE PUBLISHERS
EUGENE, OREGON

101 inspirational thoughts for mom

Text copyright © 2015 by Harvest House Publishers
Artwork copyright © by Olika Licensing, Inc./Lori Siebert

Published by Harvest House Publishers
Eugene, Oregon 97402
www.harvesthousepublishers.com

ISBN 978-0-7369-6383-1

All works of art reproduced in this book are copyrighted by Lori Siebert and may not be reproduced without the artist's permission. For more information regarding art prints featured in this book, please contact:

> Courtney Davis, Inc.
> 340 Main Street
> Franklin, Tennessee 37064
> www.courtneydavis.com

Design and production by Garborg Design Works, Savage, Minnesota

Harvest House Publishers has made every effort to trace the ownership of all poems and quotes. In the event of a question arising from the use of a poem or quote, we regret any error made and will be pleased to make the necessary correction in future editions of this book.

All Scripture verses are taken from the Holy Bible, New International Version®, NIV®. Copyright © 1973, 1978, 1984, 2011 by Biblica, Inc.® Used by permission. All rights reserved worldwide.

Printed in China

15 16 17 18 19 20 21 22 / LP / 10 9 8 7 6 5 4 3 2 1

A mother is a
mother, still the
holiest thing alive.

SAMUEL TAYLOR COLERIDGE

1 cherish this
season of your life

2

The happiest moments of my life have been the few which I have passed at home in the bosom of my family.

THOMAS JEFFERSON

3

Write it on your heart that every day is the best day in the year.

RALPH WALDO EMERSON

4

see beauty in the common

5

Beauty is but the
sensible image of
the Infinite. Like
truth and justice
it lives within us;
like virtue and
the moral law it
is a companion
of the soul.

RICHARD BANCROFT

6

When Nature's happiest touch could add no more,
Heaven lent an angel's beauty to her face.

WILLIAM JULIUS MICKLE, "MARY, QUEEN OF SCOTS"

7

*Life is made up, not of great sacrifices
or duties, but of little things, in which smiles,
and kindnesses, and small obligations, given
habitually, are what win and preserve the
heart and secure comfort.*

SIR HUMPHREY DAVY

8 rest
when
you can

9

Every house where love abides
and friendship is a guest,
is surely home, and home, sweet home;
for there the heart can rest.

HENRY VAN DYKE, "A HOME SONG"

10

drink lots
of water

11 listen wit

12

Where we
love is home,
home that
our feet may
leave, but not
our hearts.

OLIVER WENDELL
HOLMES

our heart

13

And the stars they glisten, glisten,
Seeming with bright eyes to listen
For what listen they?

JOHN KEATS

14

seek wisdom

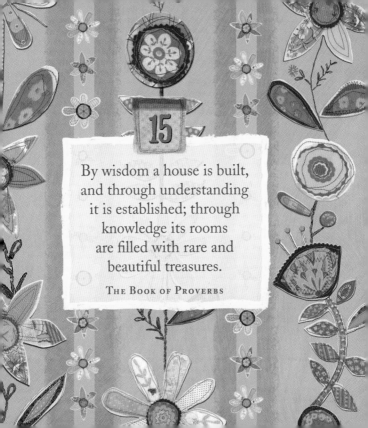

15

By wisdom a house is built,
and through understanding
it is established; through
knowledge its rooms
are filled with rare and
beautiful treasures.

THE BOOK OF PROVERBS

16

love your husband

Blessed is the influence of one true,
loving human soul on another.

George Eliot

nd let him love you

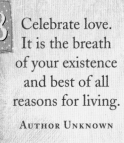

18 Celebrate love.
It is the breath
of your existence
and best of all
reasons for living.

Author Unknown

19

See your home as a safe haven

20

But what on earth is half so dear—
So longed for—as the hearth of home?

EMILY BRONTË, "A LITTLE WHILE, A LITTLE WHILE"

21

So the short journey came blithely to an end, and in the twilight she saw a group of loving faces at the door of a humble little house, which was more beautiful than any palace in her eyes, for it was home.

LOUISA MAY ALCOTT, *AN OLD-FASHIONED GIRL*

22

*Home is the one place in all this world
where hearts are sure of each other. It is the
place of confidence. It is the place where we
tear off that mask of guarded and suspicious
coldness which the world forces us to wear
in self-defense, and where we pour out
the unreserved communications of full
and confiding hearts. It is the spot where
expressions of tenderness gush out without
any sensation of awkwardness and
without any dread of ridicule.*

FREDERICK W. ROBERTSON

23

take time to be healthy

24

Everybody needs beauty as well as bread, places to play in and pray in, where nature may heal and give strength to body and soul alike.

JOHN MUIR

25

A ruffled mind makes
a restless pillow.

CHARLOTTE BRONTË

26 believe in your child

27 keep

28 Blessed are the peacemakers, for they will be called children of God.

THE BOOK OF MATTHEW

29

Home is the resort
Of love, of joy, of peace and plenty, where,
Supporting and supported, polish'd friends,
And dear relations mingle into bliss.

JAMES THOMSON

peace

30

Home is the sphere of harmony and peace,
The spot where angels find a resting place,
When, bearing blessings, they descend to earth.

SARAH JOSEPHA HALE

31 laugh big

32

Laughter is the sun that drives winter from the human face.

VICTOR HUGO

33

When the green woods laugh with the voice of joy,
And the dimpling stream runs laughing by;
When the air does laugh with our merry wit,
And the green hill laughs with the noise of it.

WILLIAM BLAKE, "LAUGHING SONG"

34

A good laugh
is sunshine in
the house.

WILLIAM
MAKEPEACE
THACKERAY

35

That day is
lost on which
one has not
laughed.

FRENCH PROVERB

36

talk to other moms

37

There is no friend like the old friend
who has shared our morning days,
no greeting like his welcome,
no homage like his praise.

OLIVER WENDELL HOLMES, "NO TIME LIKE THE OLD TIME"

38

A joy shared is a joy doubled.

JOHANN WOLFGANG
VON GOETHE

39

Of all the best
things upon earth,
I hold that a faithful
friend is the best.

OWEN MEREDITH

40

be your child's
best teacher

41

My heart is awed within me when I think
Of the great miracle that still goes on,
In silence, round me—the perpetual work
Of thy creation, finished, yet renewed
Forever. Written on thy works I read
The lesson of thy own eternity.

WILLIAM CULLEN BRYANT, "A FOREST HYMN"

42

Observe, record, tabulate, communicate. Use your five senses. Learn to see, learn to hear, learn to feel, learn to smell, and know that by practice alone you can become expert.

WILLIAM OSLER

breathe
43
deeply

44

Live in each season as it passes; breathe
the air, drink the drink, taste the fruit, and
resign yourself to the influences of each.

HENRY DAVID THOREAU

45

As the body lives by breathing,
so the soul lives by believing.

THOMAS BROOKS

46

watch
for magic
moments

47

Heaven is at the
feet of mothers.

ARABIC PROVERB

48

Of all earthly music
that which reaches
farthest into heaven
is the beating of a
truly loving heart.

HENRY WARD BEECHER

49

I wist not what to wish, yet sure thought I,
If so much excellence abide below;
How excellent is he that dwells on high?
Whose power and beauty by his works we know.
Sure he is goodness, wisdom, glory, light,
That hath this under world so richly dight.
More Heaven than Earth was here, no winter and no night.

ANNE BRADSTREET

50 believe in love

51

O man, believe in God with all your might, for hope rests on faith, love on hope, and victory on love.

JULIAN OF NORWICH

ways

52

Faith, like light, should always be simple and unbending; while love, like warmth, should beam forth on every side and bend to every necessity of our brethren.

MARTIN LUTHER

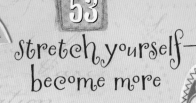

53
stretch yourself— become more

54 Represent the Lord Himself as close to you and behold how lovingly and humbly He is teaching you. Believe me, you should remain with so good a friend as long as you can. If you grow accustomed to having Him present at your side, and He sees that you do so with love and that you go about striving to please Him; He will never fail you; He will help you in all your trials; you will find Him everywhere.

SAINT TERESA OF AVILA

55

What a discovery
I made one day
that the more I
spent the more I
grew, that it was
as easy to occupy
a large place and
do much work as
an obscure place
and do little.

RALPH WALDO EMERSON

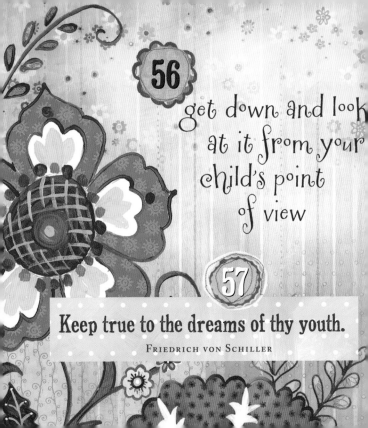

56

get down and look at it from your child's point of view

57

Keep true to the dreams of thy youth.

FRIEDRICH VON SCHILLER

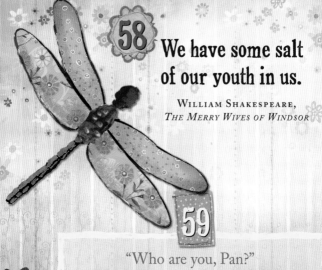

58

We have some salt of our youth in us.

WILLIAM SHAKESPEARE,
THE MERRY WIVES OF WINDSOR

59

"Who are you, Pan?"
"I am youth, Eternal Youth!
I am the Sun rising, I am Poets singing,
I am the New World. I am a little bird
That has broken out of the egg,
I am Joy, Joy, Joy."

JAMES M. BARRIE, *PETER PAN*

60

pray

61 Lord, make me an instrument of Your peace;
Where there is hatred let me sow love;
Where there is injury, pardon;
Where there is error, truth;
Where there is doubt, faith;
Where there is despair, hope;
Where there is darkness, light;
And where there is sadness, joy.

SAINT FRANCIS OF ASSISI

62

One single
grateful
thought
raised to
heaven is
the most
perfect
prayer.

G.E. LESSING

63

*Those blessings are
sweetest that are
won with prayer and
worn with thanks.*

THOMAS GOODWIN

64

be kind

65

That best portion of a good man's life;
his little, nameless, unremembered acts
of kindness and of love.

WILLIAM WORDSWORTH

6

Guard well within yourself that treasure, kindness. Know how to give without hesitation, how to lose without regret, how to acquire without meanness.

GEORGE SAND

67

let the sunshine in

69

Home is a place not only of strong affections, but of entire unreserves; it is life's undress rehearsal, its back-room, its dressing-room.

HARRIET BEECHER STOWE

70

It is in deep solitude that I find the gentleness with which I can truly love my brothers. The more solitary I am the more affection I have for them… Solitude and silence teach me to love my brothers for what they are, not for what they say.

THOMAS MERTON

71

Pray you now, forget and forgive.

WILLIAM SHAKESPEARE, *KING LEAR*

72 bless you

73

Never lose an opportunity
of seeing anything
beautiful, for beauty is
God's handwriting.

RALPH WALDO EMERSON

hild

74

let others
help you

75

give thanks

76

For stars that pierce the somber dark,
For morn, awaking with the lark,
For life new-stirring 'neath the bark,—

For sunshine and the blessed rain,
For budding grove and blossoming lane,
For the sweet silence of the plain,—

For bounty springing from the sod,
For every step by beauty trod,—
For each dear gift of joy, thank God!

FLORENCE EARLE COATES, "FOR JOY"

77

embrace the
imperfect

78

*A diamond with a flaw is worth more
than a pebble without imperfections.*

CHINESE PROVERB

79

I never expect to see
a perfect work from
imperfect man.

ALEXANDER HAMILTON

nd then be done

81

Out of the strain of the Doing,
nto the peace of the Done.

JULIA LOUISE WOODRUFF

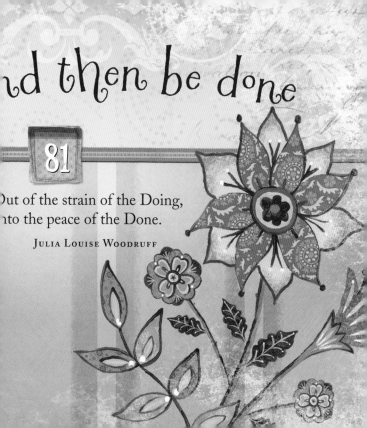

82

give in
to joy

83

Sweetest li'l feller, everybody knows;
Dunno what to call him but he's mighty lak' a rose;
Lookin' at his mammy wid eyes so shiny blue
Mek' you think that Heav'n is comin' clost ter you.

FRANK L. STANTON, "MIGHTY LAK' A ROSE"

84

A laugh, to be joyous, must flow from a joyous heart, for without kindness, there can be no true joy.

THOMAS CARLYLE

85

cry when
you need to

86

He sendeth sun, he sendeth shower,
Alike they're needful for the flower;
And joys and tears alike are sent
To give the soul fit nourishment.

SARAH FLOWER ADAMS

87

There is a comfort in the strength of love;
'Twill make a thing endurable, which else
Would overset the brain, or break the heart.

WILLIAM WORDSWORTH

88

appreciate you

89

A grandmother is a little bit parent, a little bit teacher, and a little bit best friend.

AUTHOR UNKNOWN

90

A mother is the
truest friend we have.

WASHINGTON IRVING

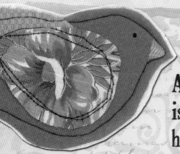

91

A mother's heart
is always with
her children.

JEWISH PROVERB

92

do a little goo

No matter what you've done for yourself or for humanity, if you can't look back on having given love and attention to your own family, what have you really accomplished?

ELBERT HUBBARD

very day

94

smile as
you go

95

A mother's happiness
is like a beacon,
lighting up the future
but reflected also on
the past in the guise
of fond memories.

HONORÉ DE BALZAC

96 *Her pleasures are in the happiness of her family.*

Jean-Jacques Rousseau

97

A happy family is but an earlier heaven.

Sir John Bowring

98

be faithful

99

As well could you expect a plant to grow without air and water as to expect your heart to grow without prayer and faith.

C.H. SPURGEON

100

Faith, mighty faith, the promise sees and looks to that alone,
Laughs at impossibilities
And cries: It shall be done.

CHARLES WESLEY

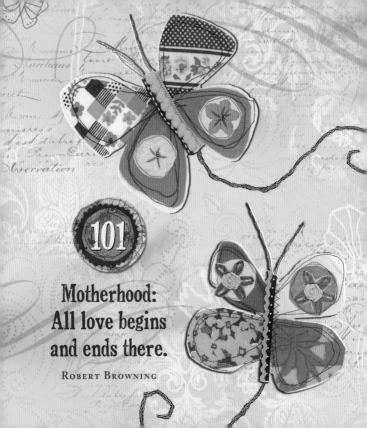

101

Motherhood:
All love begins
and ends there.

ROBERT BROWNING

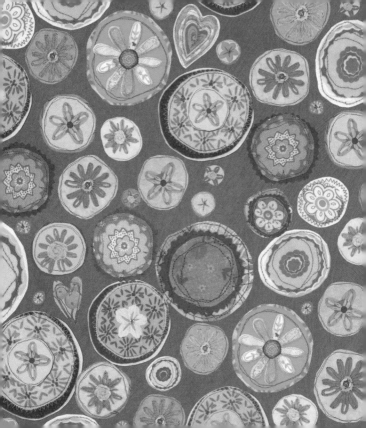

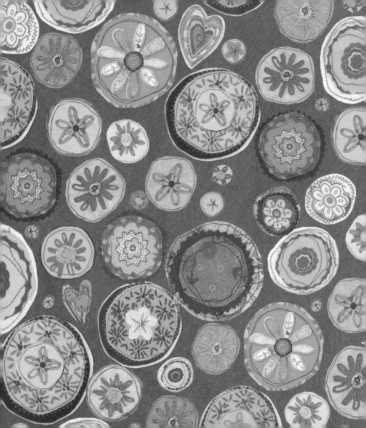